salsas
dips and relishes

RYLAND
PETERS
& SMALL

LONDON NEW YORK

salsas
dips and relishes

Elsa Petersen-Schepelern
photography by Peter Cassidy

First published in Great Britain in 2002
by Ryland Peters & Small
Kirkman House, 12–14 Whitfield Street,
London W1T 2RP
www.rylandpeters.com

10 9 8 7 6 5 4 3 2

ISBN 1 84172 252 9

A catalogue record for this book is available from
the British Library.

Printed and bound in China

Senior Designer Steve Painter
Editor Siobhan O'Connor
Production Meryl Silbert
Art Director Gabriella Le Grazie
Publishing Director Alison Starling

Food Stylist Kate Habershon
Stylist Liz Belton

Notes

All spoon measurements are level.

Preheat ovens to the specified temperature.
Recipes in this book were tested with a fan-
assisted oven. If using a regular oven, increase the
cooking times according to the manufacturer's
instructions.

Uncooked or partly cooked eggs should not be
served to the very young, the very old or frail, or
to pregnant women.

Author's acknowledgements

My thanks to my sister Kirsten and nephews Peter Bray and Luc Votan,
whose advice on this and every book is always much appreciated. Thanks
also to Sheridan Lear, the 'Preserving Princess', and mates and fellow food
writers Clare Ferguson and Alastair Hendy, this time for their help with Salsa
Verde. My thanks also go to the endlessly good-humoured Kate Habershon, for
her beautiful food styling, and to her assistant Becka Heatherston. Appreciation, as
always, to photographer Peter Cassidy who just takes my breath away, to stylist Liz Belton,
and to Steve Painter for his wonderful design, again as usual. Thanks also to Pun Kum Thai
Restaurant in Whitfield Street, London W1, who lent their authentic Thai condiment set on page 31.

contents

Salsa isn't just a dance – it's also a salad's groovy cousin or a sauce with extra pizzazz. Though we think of it as Mexican or Latin American, other countries have their own versions too. This book includes salsas, sauces and other dips from around the world – plus the sorts of quick pickles and relishes that don't require a preserving pan. Most can be made only a few minutes or an hour in advance – just enough time to develop savour and piquancy. The best thing is – they're healthy and delicious.

not just a dance ...

Avocado is a Mexican ingredient, so it tastes good in a salsa (which is, after all, a Latin American dish). Many people cut avocado into dice, but I like it scooped out with a teaspoon, all rough and creamy. Whatever you do, don't bother with any avocado except the warty-skinned, greenish-purple Hass. I grew up in an avocado-growing area and I can tell you that other varieties aren't worth the trouble.

avocado chilli salsa
with char-grilled prawns

2 red onions, quartered, then finely sliced

1 red chilli, deseeded and sliced or diced

finely grated zest and juice of 1 lime

2 large, ripe Hass avocados, halved, with pits removed*

2 ripe red tomatoes, halved, deseeded and diced

a large handful of coriander

sea salt and coarsely cracked black pepper

Char-grilled prawns

3–5 uncooked prawns per person, depending on size, with shells

2 tablespoons chilli oil

juice of 2 limes

a pinch of salt

2 tablespoons brown sugar

Serves 4

To make the salsa, put the onion, chilli and half the lime juice into a bowl and set aside to marinate for a few minutes.

Using a small teaspoon or coffee spoon, scoop out small balls of avocado into a serving bowl. Add the lime zest and remaining juice and turn gently to coat. This will stop the avocado turning brown.

Add the diced tomatoes to the onion mixture, toss gently, then add the avocado. Tear the coriander leaves over the top and sprinkle with the sea salt and black pepper. Serve the salsa with the char-grilled prawns, or with meat or chicken marinated in a chilli-olive oil marinade, then char-grilled. Warmed flour tortillas, sour cream and lettuce are also delicious accompaniments.

Char-grilled prawns Slit the prawns down the back and pull out the black vein, if any. Put the chilli oil, lime juice, salt and sugar into a bowl, add the prawns and toss to coat. Using your fingers, push the sauce into the slit and set aside for 30 minutes. Preheat a stove-top grill pan or barbecue to medium hot, add the prawns, then cook on both sides until just opaque. Serve with the avocado chilli salsa.

*Note Always prepare avocado at the last moment and coat in a little citrus juice. Avocado turns brown very quickly – don't believe the old wives' tale that the stone prevents this.

salsas

2 ears of corn, husks removed, brushed with corn oil

2 red peppers, quartered and deseeded

2 long red chillies, halved and deseeded

4 ripe red tomatoes, halved, deseeded and finely diced

1 red onion, chopped

2 garlic cloves, crushed

2 tablespoons chopped or torn coriander

Dressing

½ teaspoon sugar

1 tablespoon corn oil

juice of 1 lime

1 teaspoon salt, or to taste

freshly cracked black pepper

Barbecue spareribs

2 garlic cloves, crushed

2 tablespoons sea salt

2 tablespoons ground cumin

1 teaspoon Tabasco sauce

1 teaspoon dried oregano

125 ml honey

4 tablespoons sherry vinegar

6 tablespoons olive oil

1 kg barbecue pork spareribs

Serves 4

The Mexican habit of grilling salsa ingredients first gives them a delicious, smoky, barbecue flavour. Toasted chillies, corn, peppers and even tomatoes all benefit from a bit of fire!

mexican salsa
with barbecue spareribs

Put the corn, pepper quarters and chilli halves onto a preheated barbecue or under the grill. Toast until the pepper and chilli skins and the corn are all lightly charred. Cool, then pull off the pepper and chilli skins (leaving a few charred bits behind) and slice the kernels off the corn cob. Put into a bowl, add the tomatoes, onion and garlic, then toss well.

To make the dressing, put the sugar, corn oil, lime juice, salt and pepper into a bowl or jug, mix well, then pour over the vegetables and toss again. Cover and chill for at least 30 minutes. Before serving, stir through the chopped or torn coriander. Taste and add extra salt and freshly cracked black pepper if necessary.

Barbecue spareribs To make a marinade, put the garlic, salt, cumin, Tabasco, oregano, honey, vinegar and olive oil into a shallow dish and mix. Pat the ribs dry with kitchen paper, add them to the dish, then rub in the marinade. Cover and chill overnight.

When ready to cook, preheat the barbecue to medium, then add the ribs and cook on both sides for about 30 minutes until done. Baste from time to time with the marinade.

Cut the ribs into slices, each side of the bones, and arrange on 4 serving plates. Serve with the salsa beside or in a separate bowl. Have lots of napkins for mopping up, plus lots of cold beer.

Some people like the skin on peppers – personally, I find it indigestible and the easiest way to remove it is with a vegetable peeler. Green peppers are just unripe ordinary peppers – if you prefer ripe ones, use other colours. I love Chinese yard-long beans in salads, because they keep their crunch, but use regular beans if these are difficult to find.

green apple salsa

3 green peppers

2 Chinese yard-long beans, cut in 4, or 10 green beans

20 cm cucumber

a large handful of spring onions or 1 white onion

juice of 1½–2 oranges

2 Granny Smith apples, cored and diced

a large bunch of mint or basil, about 75 g, finely chopped (optional)

sea salt and freshly ground black pepper

Serves 4

Using a vegetable peeler, peel the peppers. Cut off the stalks and deseed. Cut into strips lengthways, then into dice, about ½ cm.

Top and tail the beans, then steam or microwave until cooked but still crisp. Plunge immediately into cold water and run the cold water until the beans are quite cool. Pat dry and cut into dice.

Cut the cucumber in half lengthways and scrape out the seed section. This is very sour and liquid, so I like it removed, but this is optional. Cut the cucumber into strips, then into dice.

Cut the spring onions into short dice or, if using a white onion, cut into ½ cm dice.

Put the peppers, beans, cucumber and spring onions or onion into a bowl, squeeze over the orange juice, then sprinkle with salt and pepper. Set aside for at least 30 minutes to develop the flavour. Just before serving, add the diced apple and toss to coat with the juice.

Serve as is, or shred the mint or basil, sprinkle over the top, then serve. This salsa is an excellent accompaniment for duck, char-grilled pork chops or chunks of boiled ham.

Sweet fruits, hot chillies and scented herbs make a great salsa combination. Papaya is wonderful because it's rich and creamy, but mango, pineapple and other tropical fruits such as lychees would also be delicious.

papaya chilli salsa
with char-grilled tuna

1 fresh ripe papaya

1 red pepper

1 yellow pepper

1 red chilli, deseeded and chopped

1 tablespoon grated fresh ginger

a large handful of coriander leaves, torn

finely grated zest and juice of 3 limes

sea salt and freshly ground black pepper

Char-grilled tuna

4 small tuna steaks or 2 large

2 tablespoons peanut oil

1 tablespoon lemon juice

1 red chilli, finely chopped

lime wedges, to serve

Serves 4

To prepare the tuna, put it into a bowl and sprinkle with the oil, lemon juice and chilli. Toss to coat and let marinate while you prepare and marinate the salsa.

To make the salsa, peel the papaya and peppers with a vegetable peeler. Cut them in half and remove the seeds. Chop into 1 cm dice. Put into a bowl, then add the chilli and ginger. Stir in the coriander, lime zest and juice, salt and pepper. Set aside for 30 minutes before serving.

When ready to cook, pat the tuna dry with kitchen paper. Preheat a stove-top grill pan, then cook very quickly on both sides until barred with brown stripes, but still pink in the middle. Don't overcook the tuna or it will be dry and tasteless.

Serve on heated dinner plates with the salsa and wedges of lime.

Breathtakingly simple, but gorgeous in taste, serve this salsa as an accompaniment for meat, fish or poultry, on pizza, or crushed onto bruschetta. Best of all is with these sweet little lamb cutlets. I like to spoon the salsa into a small bowl on the plate, with the cutlets beside. This is great food for an outdoor party – the cutlets can be eaten with the fingers and the salsa with a teaspoon.

roasted tomato and oregano salsa
with lamb cutlets

12 plum tomatoes, about 4 cm diameter

4 sprigs of oregano

5 tablespoons extra virgin olive oil

2 garlic cloves, finely sliced

2 tablespoons balsamic vinegar

a pinch of sea salt flakes, crushed

1 teaspoon harissa paste or a dash of Tabasco sauce

brown sugar (optional)

1 tablespoon freshly cracked black peppercorns

Lamb cutlets

12 lamb cutlets, frenched and chined, then all fat removed

olive oil, for frying

sea salt and freshly ground black pepper

a few oregano leaves, to serve

Serves 4

Prick the tomatoes once each with a cocktail stick. Put the tomatoes and oregano into a plastic bag with 2 tablespoons of the olive oil and the garlic. Shake to coat with oil, then transfer to a roasting tin and roast in a preheated oven at 200°C (400°F) Gas 6 until half collapsed, with the tomato skins split and slightly browned, about 30 minutes, depending on the size of the tomatoes. Brown under the grill if necessary.

To make the dressing, put the balsamic vinegar into a bowl, add the remaining olive oil, the salt and harissa or Tabasco and beat with a fork. Add brown sugar to taste, if using, and stir to dissolve. Put the tomatoes into small serving bowls, pour over the dressing and sprinkle with the pepper. Keep them warm in the turned-off oven while you fry the cutlets.

To cook the cutlets, put the oil into a frying pan, heat well, then add the cutlets, in batches if necessary, and sprinkle with salt. Fry at a high heat for about 1–2 minutes on each side until browned but still pink in the middle. Divide the cutlets between 4 heated dinner plates and add the small bowls of tomatoes. Sprinkle with oregano, salt and cracked black pepper. Serve with small spoons to eat the tomatoes.

Note Roast the tomatoes on the vines if you prefer. Some people think tomatoes on the vine have more flavour – I think they just cost more.

Thai pesto is usually used as a topping for the fish before it's cooked, but I prefer the fresh, bright tastes when it's uncooked. The solution – serve it as a salsa accompaniment. Salmon isn't an Asian fish, but its creamy richness goes very well with the sweet, hot, scented flavours of South-east Asia.

thai pesto with fish fillets

15 g mint or Asian basil (not regular basil), torn

2 stalks of lemongrass, finely sliced

2 garlic cloves, crushed

2 teaspoons fish sauce

1 tablespoon freshly squeezed lime juice

4 tablespoons peanut oil

1 tablespoon Thai sweet chilli sauce

90 g coriander, torn

To serve

4–8 fish fillets, such as salmon

peanut oil, for cooking

salad leaves, to serve

Serves 4

To make the pesto, tear up the coriander. Put the mint or basil, lemongrass, garlic, fish sauce and lime juice into a blender or food processor and blend until coarsely chopped. With the motor running, add the peanut oil and chilli sauce. (Alternatively, use a mortar and pestle.) Scoop into a bowl and stir in the coriander.

Brush the salmon with the oil. Heat a stove-top grill pan until hot, add the fish skin side down and cook for 2–3 minutes or until the fish can easily be moved in the pan. Turn it over and cook the other side for about 1 minute – the fish should still be pink in the middle. Top with the pesto and serve with salad leaves.

three raitas with naan

Raita is the Indian version of a salsa, mixed with yoghurt dressing. Serve with chunks of naan bread or with fiery curries – yoghurt and other dairy foods are able to cool the fires of chilli burns because the chemicals in chillies are fat-soluble, not water-soluble. Drinking water or beer won't cool the burn, but yoghurt will. It's a particularly healthful ingredient – and can be low-fat, too, if you like.

The first recipe, using yoghurt and mint, is a common combination, but in India, of course, they can't resist adding chillies. I like just a little – but please yourself (and your guests!)

The second combination of onion, tomato, chillies and cucumber makes a great salsa by itself, but when bathed in yoghurt, it's creamy and delicious and the sauce turns a pretty blush pink.

The third is made with cucumber: cucumber and yoghurt make one of the classic flavour combinations – a popular cooling food, especially as an accompaniment to chilli dishes.

chilli and mint

leaves from a large bunch of mint

1 teaspoon salt

½ teaspoon sugar

250 ml plain yoghurt

1 green chilli, finely sliced

Makes about 500 ml

Put the mint into a food processor and blend until finely chopped. Add the salt, sugar and yoghurt and blend briefly. Transfer to a bowl and serve, sprinkled with the sliced green chilli.

tomato, onion and chilli

250 ml yoghurt

1 teaspoon salt

1 teaspoon sugar

juice of ½ lemon

1 red onion, finely diced

1 tomato, deseeded and chopped

5 cm cucumber, halved, deseeded and chopped*

1 fresh red chilli, chopped

1 fresh green chilli, chopped

Makes about 500 ml

Put the yoghurt, salt, sugar and lemon juice into a bowl and mix to dissolve the sugar. Add the onion, tomato and chillies, stir gently, chill for 30 minutes, then serve.

cucumber and ginger

250 ml yoghurt

2 cm fresh ginger, peeled and grated

1 teaspoon sea salt

1 tablespoon sugar

1 tablespoon lemon juice

½ teaspoon ground turmeric

5 cm cucumber*

Makes about 500 ml

Put the yoghurt, ginger, salt, sugar, lemon juice and turmeric into a bowl and mix to dissolve the sugar.

Cut the ends off the cucumber, cut it in half lengthways and scrape out the seeds with a teaspoon. If the skin is tough or waxed, peel it off: otherwise leave it on. Cut the cucumber into matchstick strips, put into a bowl and pour over the yoghurt dressing. Chill for about 30 minutes, then serve.

Note If you have time, sprinkle the prepared, deseeded cucumber with salt and set aside to drain for at least 10 minutes. Rinse and pat dry with kitchen paper before using. This will remove some of the bitter juices which would otherwise seep into the dressing.

12 dried New Mexico chillies

125 ml sunflower oil

3 garlic cloves

1 tablespoon chopped fresh oregano

6 large, ripe tomatoes, skinned and deseeded

sea salt salt

corn chips, to serve

Makes about 500 ml

Break the chillies in half and remove the seeds. Heat the oil in a frying pan, add the chillies and fry until they turn bright red. Remove with a slotted spoon and put into a bowl. Cover with water and let soak for about 30 minutes.

Add the garlic to the pan and fry until golden. Transfer to a food processor, add the drained chillies and chop coarsely. Add the oregano and tomatoes and chop again. Add salt and pepper to taste and serve with corn chips. Alternatively, serve as an all-purpose sauce for the table – add it to any dish.

salsa roja with corn chips

Mexican salsas aren't just chopped fresh salads. Mexico, too, has the 'sauce' kind of salsa – versions of this one can be found on restaurant and diner tables all over the country. Add it to anything you think needs a bit of livening up, or serve with corn chips and lots of Margaritas. New Mexico chillies have a smoky, earthy flavour, but aren't overly hot.

salsa verde
with soft-boiled eggs and baby leeks

3 tablespoons capers in salt

2 cups fresh parsley leaves

2 garlic cloves, crushed

3 anchovy fillets

6 tablespoons olive oil

½ tablespoon sherry vinegar

To serve

250 g baby leeks

6 small eggs

sea salt and freshly
ground black pepper

Serves 6

I find many salsa verde recipes too violently sour, but this one is smooth and delicious, and goes with any mild-tasting foods. Friend and fellow food writer, Alastair Hendy, serves it with leeks: it's also good with eggs and with poached chicken breasts.

To make the salsa verde, put the capers into a bowl, add water and let soak to remove the salt, about 10–15 minutes, changing the water at least once. Pour off the water and remove the capers, leaving the salt behind.

Put the parsley into a small food processor and chop coarsely. Add the capers, garlic and anchovies and chop again. Add 4 tablespoons of the olive oil and the vinegar, blend again and taste. Add the remaining olive oil if preferred – the sauce should be thick and paste-like, not liquid.

Meanwhile, cut the leeks down two-thirds of their length, leaving them attached at the root end. Cut again into quarters and wash thoroughly to remove all grit and sand. Transfer to a steamer and steam until tender, about 5–10 minutes (the time depends on the size of the leeks).

Put the eggs into a small saucepan of cold water and bring to the boil: from the point of boiling, time them for 4 minutes. Drain and run under cold water to stop them cooking further. Drain again and tap all over to crack the shells. Gently peel off the shells (carefully, because the eggs will be soft). Carefully cut them in half lengthways and put onto a serving platter. Drain the leeks and add them to the platter. Serve the salsa verde spooned over the leeks, or transfer to a separate bowl.

tabbouleh in party pitas

125 g medium bulghur

a very large bunch of
flat leaf parsley

a very large bunch of mint

2 large, ripe tomatoes,
halved and deseeded

3 spring onions, sliced

2 tablespoons extra virgin olive oil

1 tablespoon freshly squeezed
lemon juice

sea salt and cracked black pepper

Chilli sauce

1 teaspoon harissa paste
or 2 dashes Tabasco sauce

4 tablespoons olive oil

sea salt

Party pitas

20 mini pita breads

1 quantity of hoummus (page 43)

125 ml plain yoghurt

*15 cm squares of greaseproof
paper, folded into cones*

Serves 20 as party food or 4 as an accompaniment

Tabbouleh is a great Lebanese classic salad – it should be green, with tons of parsley and mint (there should be so much green that you hardly notice the bulghur or tomatoes). Here, it's served as party food in mini pita breads with a dollop of hoummus and homemade chilli sauce in a separate bowl for people to help themselves. It's also great with kebabs and felafel.

To make the tabbouleh, soak the bulghur in water for 20 minutes, then drain. Coarsely chop the parsley and mint.

Put the tomatoes, chopped herbs, spring onions and bulghur into a bowl. Sprinkle with the oil and lemon juice, add salt and pepper to taste and toss well.

To make the chilli sauce, put the harissa paste or Tabasco into a dipping bowl, add the olive oil and stir well. Add salt to taste.

Party pitas Heat the pitas in a microwave or in the oven according to the packet instructions. Cut in half. Add a teaspoon of hoummus to each pocket and another teaspoon of plain yoghurt. Top with the tabbouleh and serve wrapped in little greaseproof paper cones with the dipping bowl of chilli sauce for people to help themselves.

red pesto

Ordinary green pesto can be expensive to make unless you grow your own basil or have a proper vegetable market nearby where you can buy it by the armful, rather than in dinky little packages from the supermarket. Red pesto, on the other hand, is easy to make, as long as you have sun-dried tomatoes on hand. This recipe is a thousand times better than the store-bought version. Serve it in the usual way, as a sauce stirred through pasta, cooked on top of pizza, on mini toasts as party food or as a flavour-enhancer in meat or poultry sauces.

90 g sun-dried tomatoes

40 g pine nuts

4 tablespoons freshly grated Parmesan cheese

125 ml olive oil

Makes about 375 ml

Put the sun-dried tomatoes into a bowl, cover with 250 ml boiling water and let soak overnight. Drain, reserving the liquid for another use (such as adding flavour to soups and stews). Chop the tomatoes with scissors.

Put the pine nuts into a dry frying pan and heat gently until golden. Take care – they burn easily. Remove from the pan and let cool.

Put the nuts into a blender and blend to a meal. Add the drained tomatoes and Parmesan and blend again. Slowly drizzle in the olive oil to form a thick paste.

palm sugar

1 cylinder palm sugar or
2 tablespoons brown sugar

If using palm sugar
(available from Asian
stores), put it on a board
and shave off shards with
a knife – enough to half-
fill a small bowl.

red chilli flakes

a large handful of large
red dried chillies

Put the chillies into a
dry frying pan and heat
gently until aromatic.
Take care, because
they burn easily.

Using a small food
processor or mortar and
pestle, crush into flakes.
To be authentic, keep
the seeds in the mixture,
but, if you prefer, you
can remove as many
as possible before
crushing. Serve the
flakes in a small bowl.

chilli fish sauce

3 fresh red bird's eye
chillies, finely sliced
crossways

125 ml fish sauce

Put the sliced chillies and
fish sauce into a bowl,
stir briefly, then transfer
to a small bowl.

chilli vinegar sauce

125 ml white rice vinegar

3 fresh green bird's eye
chillies, finely sliced
crossways

Put the vinegar and
chillies into a small jar,
shake to mix, then set
aside. When ready to
serve, transfer to a
small bowl.

thai condiments

South-east Asian homes and restaurants don't usually keep salt and pepper on the
table. Instead, they have a 'cruet' of condiments, such as this one from Thailand.
They include toasted dried red chilli flakes, sugar – usually palm sugar – and chillies
steeped in fish sauce and vinegar, plus a separate bowl of chopped peanuts. Serve
these condiments as great accompaniments for many Thai dishes, including noodles.

dips and relishes

vietnamese spring rolls
with pickles and dipping sauce

60 g beanthread noodles
(2 bundles)

1 package Vietnamese ricepaper
wrappers (*bahn trang*)

1 butterhead lettuce,
leaves finely shredded

a large bunch of Vietnamese
herbs, such as coriander and mint

Chinese barbecued pork,
duck or shrimp*

Pickled carrots and radishes

1–2 carrots

about 10 radishes

2 teaspoons rice vinegar

2 pinches of salt

4 teaspoons sugar

Nuòc cham dipping sauce

1 garlic clove, crushed

½ hot red chilli, finely chopped

1 tablespoon sugar

juice from 1 wedge of lime

2 tablespoons fish sauce

Serves 4

Vietnam has produced one of the world's truly great cuisines – fresh with salads and herbs, and less oily than Chinese. This recipe includes several of its greatest components; fresh pickles and a sublime dipping sauce.

To make the pickles, peel the carrots and cut into long, thin strips with a vegetable peeler. Roll up and cut into thin strips. Alternatively, slice on a mandoline. Finely slice the radishes on a mandoline – aim for see-through slices. Put the carrots into one bowl and the radishes into another. Divide the vinegar, salt and sugar between the bowls, then add 125 ml water to each one. Set aside for at least 15 minutes or up to 24 hours. Drain before using.

To make the dipping sauce, grind the garlic, chilli and sugar to a paste using a mortar and pestle. Add the lime juice, fish sauce and 2½ tablespoons water.

Soak the beanthread noodles in hot water for 15 minutes, then drain and keep in cold water until ready to serve.

To prepare the spring rolls, dip 1 ricepaper sheet in a dish of water for about 30 seconds until softened. Put onto a plate (not a board, or they will dry out). On one side of the sheet, put a few shreds of lettuce, noodles, herbs, pork, duck or shrimp, and pickled carrot and radish. There should be lots of herbs.

Roll up the ricepaper like a cigar and repeat until all the ingredients have been used. Put the rolls on a serving platter, spray with a mist of water and cover with a damp cloth or kitchen paper until ready to serve. To serve, spray with water again and serve with the dipping sauce. Alternatively, serve the ingredients on separate plates for guests to assemble their own rolls.

*Note If unavailable, rub 2 duck breasts with Chinese five-spice powder and let marinate for 15 minutes. Transfer to a preheated frying pan, skin side down, and cook for about 10 minutes until the skin is crisp, the fat runs and the flesh is cooked half through. Turn them over and cook the other side until medium rare. Set aside, let cool, then shred or slice finely.

chinese spiced salt

1 tablespoon Szechuan peppercorns

1 tablespoon red peppercorns

1 tablespoon white peppercorns

1 tablespoon green peppercorns

1 tablespoon black peppercorns

4 tablespoons sea salt flakes

Makes about 125 ml

Put the peppercorns into a dry frying pan and heat gently to release the aromas. Transfer to a blender or mortar and pestle, add the salt and blend briefly until coarsely crushed. Transfer to a small dipping bowl and serve.

*Note To make chips, cut them to your preferred size, soak in iced water for 20 minutes, rinse and pat dry with kitchen paper. Fry first at 180°C (350°F) until pale gold, then drain, increase the heat to 195°C (385°F) and fry for a few minutes more or until golden brown. Drain on kitchen paper, sprinkle with salt, then serve.

chubby chips with ...

The classic accompaniments for chips* are salt, vinegar and mayonnaise. These three fiery dips are spicy variations on those classics and are also terrific with other dishes, such as rare roast beef, char-grilled prawns or party foods of many kinds. Cook skinny chips if you like, but I like mine of a more substantial nature.

wasabi mayonnaise

2 egg yolks

1 extra whole egg (if using a food processor)

2 tablespoons lemon juice

½ teaspoon Dijon mustard

a pinch of sea salt

250 ml cold-pressed oil, such as sunflower (not olive)

3–4 tablespoons wasabi paste (1 tube)

Makes about 500 ml

Put the egg yolks and whole egg into a food processor, add the lemon juice, mustard, a pinch of salt and 4 tablespoons of the oil. Turn on the machine and blend until creamy, a few seconds. Add the remaining oil, a tablespoon at a time, drizzling in slowly. Add in stages, not in a thin stream as most books advise.

When all the oil has been added, if the mixture is too thick, add a teaspoon or so of warm water.

Stir in the wasabi paste just before serving.

chilli lemongrass vinegar

500 ml white rice vinegar or cider vinegar

4 stalks of lemongrass, trimmed and sliced lengthways

2 fresh red chillies, such as serrano, sliced lengthways and deseeded

1 bottle, 500 ml, sterilized

Makes 500 ml

Put the vinegar into a stainless steel saucepan and warm gently. Put the lemongrass and chillies into the prepared bottle. Using a funnel, fill the bottle with the warmed vinegar. Let cool before sealing with a cork.

Keep the bottle on the windowsill for 7–14 days, then use immediately or strain into a clean, sterilized bottles.

Make this tapenade with green or black olives – the best quality you can find. Use it (and the marmalade on the next page) as a topping for thinly sliced, toasted baguettes or black bread and serve with drinks before dinner.

toasted baguettes with **tapenade**

250 g green or black olives, pitted

1 tablespoon capers in salt, or caperberries, rinsed and patted dry

3 anchovy fillets, rinsed and chopped

1 tablespoon freshly squeezed lemon juice

1½ tablespoons extra virgin olive oil

sliced baguette, bruschetta or Melba toast, to serve

Makes about 250 ml

Using a mortar and pestle, grind the pitted olives, capers or caperberries and anchovies into a paste. Add the olive oil in a thin stream, then add the lemon juice. Alternatively, use a small blender.

Serve with thin slices of baguette, or on bruschetta or Melba toast.

4 tablespoons olive oil

1 kg red onions, finely sliced

1 bay leaf

2 chillies, deseeded and finely
sliced (optional)

1 tablespoon sugar

1 tablespoon red wine vinegar

a pinch of salt

1 tablespoon crème de cassis

a pinch of ground allspice

small pieces of toast, to serve

Makes about 250 ml

red onion marmalade

Heat the oil in a heavy frying pan, add the onions, bay leaf, chillies, if using, and sugar, and stir-fry until the onions start to soften. Cover with a lid and let steam for about 15 minutes so the onions will soften.

Remove the lid and continue cooking on a low heat for about 30 minutes until almost melted. Add the vinegar, salt, crème de cassis and allspice.

Continue cooking gently until the onions have become thick and jam-like. Remove from the heat, let cool, then keep in a lidded container in the refrigerator until ready to use. Serve on small toasts with drinks.

You can make this marmalade with ordinary onions, but red onions, red wine vinegar and crème de cassis will make for a rosy result. Use the rest of the bottle of crème de cassis to make Kir Royales to serve with the toasts.

baba ganoush

Baba ganoush is the famous creamy aubergine purée with smoky overtones. It's best to char them over an open fire or barbecue to achieve the authentic smoky flavour, but, if you don't have one, a hot grill or the open flame on a gas stove are also fine. Serve baba ganoush as a dip for parties or with other dishes as a first course.

3 aubergines

4 tablespoons plain yoghurt

2 tablespoons tahini paste

1 garlic clove, crushed

1 teaspoon salt

juice of 1–2 lemons, to taste

1 tablespoon chopped fresh
flat leaf parsley (optional)

pita breads, warmed or
lightly toasted, to serve

Serves 8

Put the aubergines on top of the open gas flame on top of the stove and cook until well charred on all sides. The steam created inside the vegetable will cook the flesh. The aubergines must be charred all over and soft in the middle. Remove from the flame and let cool on a plate.

When cool, carefully pull off the skins and stems. Don't leave any charred bits. Put the flesh into a bowl, then blend with a hand-held stick blender or potato masher: the texture should not be too smooth. Add the yoghurt, tahini, garlic and salt and blend again.

Add the juice of 1 lemon, taste, then gradually add more juice until you achieve flavour and texture to your taste. Transfer to a serving bowl and sprinkle with finely chopped parsley, if using.

Serve with wedges of toasted pita breads for scooping the dip.

hoummus
with flat beans

I serve this unusual combination with drinks before dinner. People are always surprised, but then have to be prevented from overdosing on it, in order to leave room for the rest of the meal.

1 cup dried chickpeas

1 teaspoon salt

6 tablespoons tahini paste

125 ml freshly squeezed lemon juice, about 2–3 lemons

2 garlic cloves, crushed

salt, to taste

To serve

1 tablespoon olive oil

1 teaspoon harissa paste or paprika

a handful of flat beans or runner beans, sliced diagonally into 5 cm pieces

Serves 6

Put the chickpeas into a saucepan and cover with 750 ml boiling water. Soak for 12 hours or overnight.

When ready to cook, drain the chickpeas, transfer to a saucepan, cover with fresh water and bring to the boil. Reduce the heat and simmer gently until almost tender (the time will depend on the age of the beans and where they were grown). When almost done, add 1 teaspoon salt and simmer until soft. Drain, reserving a little of the cooking water. (Do not add salt at the beginning of the cooking time or the beans will stay tough.)

Drain the beans and transfer to a food processor. Purée until smooth, then press through a sieve or food mill to remove the remains of the tough skins.

Stir in the tahini paste and lemon juice, then the crushed garlic. Taste and add salt or extra lemon juice to taste, and a little of the cooking water, until you achieve a creamy purée.

Spoon into a bowl and make a swirl with a teaspoon. Put the olive oil and harissa or paprika into a cup, stir well, then pour the mixture into the swirls. Put the bowl on a serving dish, add the flat beans or runner beans, then serve.

125 ml peanut or sunflower oil

1 tablespoon mustard seeds

2 red onions, diced or sliced

3 garlic cloves, crushed

2 tablespoons grated fresh ginger

about 500 g fresh okra, trimmed and cut crossways into 1 cm chunks

sea salt and freshly ground black pepper

1–2 small, mild green chillies, sliced (optional)

Onion and mustard seed relish

4 tablespoons peanut or sunflower oil

1 tablespoon mustard seeds

1 onion, coarsely grated or chopped

3 cm fresh ginger, grated

4 garlic cloves, crushed

½–1 teaspoon ground turmeric

a pinch of salt, or to taste

Serves 4

This mustard seed relish is a variation on a traditional Indian technique called 'tempering'. The relish is added to many dishes as a last-minute flavour-enhancer. When served separately, it's great as a topping for grilled meat and poultry. The cooked salsa is also based on an Indian vegetarian dish, and Indian cooks have solved the age-old dilemma of how to stop okra juices turning to ooze. The secret is never to let a single drop of water touch them at any stage of cooking. Before cooking okra, wash and pat very dry with kitchen paper, then let dry completely before cutting. If you never liked okra before, I think you'll find this dish the exception.

stir-fried okra salsa
with mustard seed relish

To make the salsa, put the oil into a frying pan over medium heat, then add the mustard seeds. Stir-fry until they pop. Add the onion, garlic and ginger and salt and pepper to taste. Stir-fry until softened and translucent. Add the okra and stir-fry until cooked but crisp, then stir in the chillies, if using

To make the onion and mustard seed relish, put the oil into a frying pan over a moderate heat. When hot, add the mustard seeds. Fry until they pop, then stir in the onion, ginger, garlic, turmeric and salt. Cook until the onion softens and browns slightly.

Serve the okra with the relish in a separate small bowl, for guests to help themselves.

6 long peppers or 8 regular,
red, yellow and orange

2–3 medium-hot chillies,
such as serrano

2 teaspoons salt

4 tablespoons extra virgin olive oil

2–4 tablespoons rice vinegar,
sherry vinegar or cider vinegar

To serve

a handful of oregano leaves

cracked black pepper

Serves 4–8,
with other dishes

Cut the peppers and chillies in half lengthways, leaving them attached at the stem end. Scrape out the membranes and seeds. Put the peppers and chillies under a preheated grill and cook until the skins are charred. Remove to a stainless steel saucepan and cover with the lid. Let steam to loosen the skins. Remove the skins, retaining any juices in the saucepan.

Arrange the peppers and chillies in a plastic container with a lid. Add any juices from the saucepan and sprinkle with the salt, oil and vinegar. Cover and set aside for 30 minutes or up to 2 days in the refrigerator.

To serve, top with the oregano and pepper and serve with antipasti, pizza or bruschetta.

pickled peppers

When grilled, peppers take on a marvellous sweet flavour – add a quick pickle of salt and vinegar and you have a deliciously bright taste. Leave out the chillies if you like your pickles cool. I prefer the smooth, mild flavour of rice vinegar, but sherry and cider vinegars are great, too. The longer you leave the mixture, the more 'pickled' it will become.

quick **pickles**

Courgettes aren't always green. Yellow ones are very sweet in flavour (there is a green-and-white striped variety, too). I particularly like the baby ones, about 5–7 cm long (both courgette and zucchini, their Italian name, mean 'little squash'), but have used slightly bigger ones for this dish.

courgettes and rosemary with pepper oil

3 green courgettes

3 yellow courgettes

salt

4 tablespoons extra virgin olive oil

a small handful of tiny sprigs of rosemary (the smallest end leaves), to serve

1–2 tablespoons peppercorns, red, black and green, cracked

shredded zest of 1 lemon

2 tablespoons cider vinegar

Red pepper oil

4 red peppers

250 ml extra virgin olive oil

Serves 4–8

To make the red pepper oil, quarter and deseed the peppers, put them on a shallow baking tray and grill, skin side up, until soft and the skins blackened. Remove from the heat and transfer to a saucepan, adding any juices from the tray. Put on the lid and set aside for a few minutes to steam off the skins. Pull or scrape off the skins, reserving any juices.

Transfer the peppers, juices and olive oil to a blender and purée until smooth. Let settle. Strain off the liquid into a bowl or jug.

Cut the courgettes into ½ cm slices lengthways. Put onto a plate and sprinkle with salt. Set aside to drain for about 30 minutes. Discard the liquid, rinse off the salt and pat dry with kitchen paper.

Put the slices into a plastic bag, add the olive oil and shake until coated. Transfer to a preheated stove-top grill pan and cook for about 3 minutes on one side, without moving them. The flesh should be barred with lines and just becoming translucent around the edges. Turn them over and cook the other side until lightly barred with brown. They should be tender, but not too soft.

Transfer to a long, shallow serving dish and sprinkle with the rosemary sprigs and cracked pepper. Sprinkle with the lemon zest and vinegar and let marinate for 30 minutes or overnight. If leaving overnight, cover and chill. Return to room temperature to serve.

Sprinkle with the pepper oil and serve as antipasti, on bruschetta or in baguettes with cheese.

These oven-dried tomatoes achieve some of the flavour of sun-dried without the leathery texture. The quick pickling effect of balsamic vinegar gives a rather sweet flavour – other vinegars such as sherry and cider give a lighter taste. Ordinary fresh sliced tomato is also great dressed simply with pepper and a sprinkle of vinegar – never mind the oil or the salt. Try it.

oven-dried tomatoes
with roasted garlic, balsamic and thyme

24 small plum tomatoes or other small tomatoes

sugar

sea salt flakes

2–3 garlic cloves, cut into fine slivers

about 2 tablespoons balsamic vinegar, to sprinkle

1 tablespoon thyme leaves

Serves 4

Halve the tomatoes crossways and cut out the dense central core with a sharp knife. Arrange apart on oven trays. On each half, put a small pinch of sugar and a few sea salt flakes. Push 2 small slivers of garlic into each half.

Roast in a preheated oven at 200°C (400°F) Gas 6 for about 20 minutes, then reduce the heat to 150°C (300°F) Gas 2 for another 10 minutes. When collapsed, soft and starting to brown, remove from the oven*.

To make a quick pickle, sprinkle them with balsamic vinegar and thyme leaves and set aside to marinate for about 30 minutes. At this point, they can be used as a topping on pizzas and bruschetta, or served as a salsa.

*Note If you cook the tomatoes for 15–30 minutes more (or longer, depending on size) at the lowest temperature, they will dry out into an approximation of sun-dried tomatoes (only, I think, better). When dried, they are good served with drinks.

You can use precooked beetroot for this dish, but, if you're cooking them yourself, make sure there aren't any cuts on the skins and don't cut off the stalk end or the thin root. If you do, all the beautiful colour will seep out into the water. Use store-bought pâté, or my recipe below.

danish spiced beetroot with pâté

1 kg small cooked beetroot

1 tablespoon cloves

1 tablespoon allspice berries, coarsely crushed

3 cinnamon sticks, broken

300 ml white wine vinegar

6–8 tablespoons sugar

Danish liver pâté

250 g chopped fatty bacon

500 g lamb's liver, trimmed and cut into 3 cm pieces

1 egg

1 teaspoon salt

2 teaspoons freshly ground black pepper

2 teaspoons ground allspice

2 anchovy fillets

1 tablespoon butter

1 tablespoon plain flour

250 ml milk

2 large onions, finely chopped

Serves about 20

Cut off the tops and bottoms of the beetroot and slip off the skins. Slice the beetroot finely – on a mandoline if you have one – then pack the slices into sterilized preserving jars (see page 59). Put the cloves, allspice and cinnamon sticks between the layers.

Put the vinegar and sugar into a small saucepan, bring to the boil and simmer until the sugar has dissolved. Pour into the jars until the beetroot are completely covered – if the jars are large, you may have to prepare more vinegar and sugar mixture.

Seal the jars and use within 7 days. Serve with pâté on light rye bread, pumpernickel, toast or wholegrain bread.

Danish liver pâté Put the bacon into a food processor and work to a paste. Remove and set aside. Put the liver into the processor and blend until smooth. Add the bacon, then the egg, salt, pepper, allspice and anchovies. Meanwhile, put the butter into a saucepan, heat until melted, then stir in the flour and cook for 1 minute. Gradually stir in the milk and cook until thickened. Cool, then stir in the onions. Add to the liver mixture in the processor and pulse briefly.

Transfer to a large terrine, cover with foil and a lid, then stand the terrine in a roasting tin. Half-fill the tin with water, then transfer to a preheated oven and cook at 200°C (400°F) Gas 6 for 20 minutes. Remove the lid and foil and bake, uncovered, for a further 20 minutes. When cooked, the pâté will shrink away from the sides of the terrine. Cool and chill overnight, then serve.

I love the salty, sour flavour of these lemons. Before you use them in a recipe, take out of the brine, remove and discard the flesh, then slice the peel and use in recipes. The peel is also good with black olives.

preserved lemons
for Moroccan chicken tagine

8 lemons

12 tablespoons sea salt

6 cloves

2 cinnamon sticks

6 cardamom pods

2 fresh bay leaves

Chicken tagine

2 pinches of saffron threads

1 whole chicken

3 cm fresh ginger, finely sliced

2 garlic cloves, finely sliced

2 tablespoons olive oil

2 large onions, grated

2 cinnamon sticks

sliced peel of 1 preserved lemon

sea salt and freshly
ground black pepper

20 black olives

Serves 4

Cut 6 of the lemons in quarters lengthways, leaving them attached at the stem end. Cram 1 tablespoon salt into the slits of each lemon and push the fruit into a preserving jar. Add the cinnamon, cardamom and bay leaves. Add the remaining 6 tablespoons salt to the jar, add the juice of the 2 remaining lemons and top up with boiling water. Seal and use after 2 weeks.

To use, remove the lemon from the brine and scrape out and discard the flesh. Use the peel cut into slices with chicken tagines and other stews.

Chicken tagine with preserved lemons Soak the saffron in 4 tablespoons boiling water for 30 minutes. Make slits in the breast of the chicken and insert slivers of ginger and garlic. Heat the oil in a large casserole dish, add the chicken and brown on all sides until golden. Add the onions, saffron and its soaking water, cinnamon sticks and the preserved lemon peel. Add 250 ml water, a pinch of salt and freshly ground black pepper. Cover with a lid, bring to the boil and simmer on top of the stove or cook in a preheated oven at 150°C (300°F) Gas 2 until tender. Stir in the olives and serve.

Alternatively, add the lemon and olives for the last 10 minutes of cooking (this is the traditional way).

I am a great fan of curds – they're delicious in tarts, good on toast and hellishly decadent with croissants. I use mango purée from India to make this – but you could use fresh mango (just make sure it's superbly ripe and sweet) or frozen mango, blended to a purée.

mango and ginger curd
with croissants

250 ml mango purée

5 cm fresh ginger, peeled and grated

grated zest of 1 lime and` freshly squeezed of ½ lime

160 g sugar

75 g unsalted butter, cut into cubes

4 large eggs, beaten

freshly baked croissants, brioche, or toast, to serve

Makes about 750 ml

Put the mango, ginger, lime zest, lime juice and sugar into a non-reactive (stainless steel or enamel) saucepan and heat until simmering. Simmer for about 5 minutes, then strain into a heatproof bowl. Discard the residue.

Put the bowl over a saucepan of gently simmering water and add the butter. Stir until melted.

Strain the eggs through a fine sieve into the bowl and stir well. Cook gently, stirring often at the beginning, then continuously at the end until the mixture coats the back of a spoon, about 45 minutes. Do not let boil or the mixture will curdle.

Remove from the heat and pour into warm, sterilized preserving jars (see page 59). Seal and let cool. Use immediately with croissants, or store in the refrigerator for up to 1 week.

sweet things

This sauce is based on a delicious lemon and passionfruit curd. Mix it with 3 tablespoon crème fraîche and churn into an ice cream, or dilute with lemon juice and rum to make this wonderful sauce.

passionfruit and rum sauce
with ice cream

4 large, ripe passionfruit

1 teaspoon finely grated lemon zest and the freshly squeezed juice of 1 lemon

75 g unsalted butter, cut into cubes

250 g caster sugar

3 large eggs, beaten

To serve

½ tablespoon caster sugar

2 tablespoons white rum

vanilla ice cream

Makes about 750 ml

Cut the tops off the passionfruit and scoop the pulp and seeds into a bowl.

Put the lemon zest, lemon juice, butter and sugar into a heatproof bowl set over a saucepan of gently simmering water. Don't let the base of the bowl touch the water.

Heat gently, stirring, until the sugar dissolves and the butter melts.

Strain the eggs through a fine sieve into the bowl and stir well. Cook gently, stirring often at the beginning, then continuously at the end until the mixture coats the back of a spoon, about 30–40 minutes. Do not let boil or the mixture will curdle.

Remove from the heat and stir in the passionfruit pulp. Pour into warm sterilized jars.* Seal and let cool. Use immediately or store in the refrigerator for up to 1 week.

When ready to serve, mix the caster sugar and rum to dissolve the sugar, then stir 1 tablespoon of the mixture into the curd. Add the remaining mixture, a little at a time, until you reach a pouring consistency. Spoon the sauce over the ice cream and serve.

*Sterilizing preserving jars Wash the jars in hot, soapy water and rinse in boiling water. Put into a large saucepan and cover with hot water. With the lid on, bring the water to the boil and continue boiling for 15 minutes. Turn off the heat, then leave the jars in the hot water until just before they are to be filled. Invert the jars onto a clean cloth to dry. Sterilize the lids for 5 minutes, by boiling or according to the manufacturer's instructions. The jars should be filled and sealed while they are still hot. For useful guidelines on preserving, see website http://hgic.clemson.edu/factsheets/HGIC3040.htm.

Peanut butter is the easiest thing in the world to make yourself. Make it with other nuts, such as the cashews here, and it's even more interesting. The chocolate-bitter flavour contrasts nicely with the cinnamon toast. If you like your nut butter sweeter, by all means add some sugar, but try it like this first. This recipe makes a smooth butter – if you like some crunch, reserve some of the nuts, chop coarsely, then stir them in at the end.

chocolate cashew butter
with cinnamon toast

1 cup unsalted cashew nuts

a small pinch of salt

1½–3 tablespoons safflower oil

6 squares cooking chocolate, with 70 per cent cocoa butter

Cinnamon toast

8 thick slices of bread

caster sugar

ground cinnamon

Serves 4

To make the nut butter, put the nuts and salt into a blender or food processor and grind until smooth. With the motor running, drizzle in the oil in a thin stream until creamy. You may have to scrape down the sides of the bowl.

Put the chocolate into a bowl and microwave on HIGH for about 1 minute, or until softened. Alternatively, melt in a heatproof bowl set over a saucepan of gently simmering water. Scrape the chocolate into the nut mixture and blend again. I like the butter more runny – add a little extra oil to achieve this. Chill the cashew butter until ready to serve.

Cinnamon toast Put the bread under a preheated grill and toast on one side only. Put the sugar and cinnamon into a bowl, mix evenly, then dust over the other side. Grill that side until the sugar melts and the mixture is brown. Serve with a bowl of chocolate cashew butter.

This glorious sauce comes from Denmark, where it is made with raspberries (*hindbaer*) or strawberries (*jordbaer*). My mother used it as a sauce for Danish Christmas rice pudding, a creamy rice concoction I liked much better than the ordinary baked version. In any case, use this sauce with ice cream and other creamy puddings, or add more juice and churn it into a sorbet.

red berry sauce
for waffles and ice cream

2 punnets raspberries or strawberries

freshly squeezed juice of ½ small lemon

75 g sugar

2 teaspoons cornflour

2 teaspoons brandy

strawberry or raspberry ice cream, or sweetened whipped cream, to serve

Crispy waffles

230 g plain flour

¼ teaspoon salt

½ tablespoon baking powder

2 eggs, separated

250 ml milk

1 tablespoon butter, melted

Serves 4

If using raspberries, pick them over. If using strawberries, wash them, pat dry on kitchen paper, then hull them. Put the berries and lemon juice into a saucepan, add the sugar and bring to the boil, stirring often. Simmer until the juice has come out of the berries, then strain through a fine sieve, pushing through as much pulp as possible. Discard the residue.

Taste the juice and add more sugar to taste. Mix the cornflour in a bowl with 2 teaspoons water until smooth (this is called 'slaking'). Reheat the juice and stir in the cornflour. Cook, stirring constantly, until the juice is slightly thickened and clear (the cornflour makes it clear and sparkling). Cool, then stir in the brandy. Serve with waffles topped with ice cream or whipped cream.

Crispy waffles Sift the flour, salt and baking powder into a bowl and make a well in the centre. Beat the egg yolks until creamy. Put the egg whites into a second bowl and whisk until stiff and frothy. Pour the melted butter into the flour, then the egg yolks and milk. Mix well, then fold in the beaten egg whites.

Heat the waffle iron until smoking (or as recommended by the manufacturer), pour a little batter into each compartment and spread over quickly. Cook as directed by the manufacturer, then transfer the waffle to a heated plate and cook the remaining mixture in the same way. If using a large, electric waffle iron, break the waffles into segments, then serve. The waffles can be kept in a warm oven for about 20 minutes. They can also be frozen and reheated from frozen in a preheated oven at 180°C (350°F) Gas 4 for 10 minutes.

index